Issues Raised During the Army After Next Spring Wargame

Walter L. Perry, Bruce R. Pirnie, John V. Gordon IV

Prepared for the United States Army

Arroyo Center

RAND

For more information on the RAND Arroyo Center, contact the Director of Operations, (310) 393-0411, extension 6500, or visit the Arroyo Center's Web site at http://www.rand.org/organization/ard/

The Army After Next (AAN) project, led by the U.S. Army Training and Doctrine Command (TRADOC), was initiated by the Chief of Staff of the Army (CSA) in February 1996. The project's goals are to link Army XXI to a long-term vision of the Army extending well into the next century, and to ensure that this vision informs evolving Army research and development requirements. At the request of the TRADOC's Deputy Chief of Staff for Doctrine (DCSDOC), RAND Arroyo Center is supporting TRADOC in this effort.

As part of the AAN project, TRADOC is conducting a series of high-level wargames to explore issues affecting the development of the U.S. Army after about 2010. The 1998 Spring Wargame is the third game in the series. All of these games have been held at the Center for Strategic Leadership at the Army War College. The Arroyo Center's role in the 1998 Spring Wargame is to assist TRADOC by (1) participating with the TRADOC Analysis Center (TRAC) in the development of the wargame Analysis Plan; (2) identifying the issues, derived from the game objectives, that were explored in the game; (3) participating with TRAC in the development of the Emerging Impressions Report; and (4) assessing game results.

This report documents the Arroyo Center's analysis of the data collected during the game, and information gathered from various sources since the completion of the game, including our Initial Impressions Report (PM-809-A) and TRAC's Emerging Impressions Report to TRADOC. This report analyzes major issues and insights arising from the game and offers recommendations to improve the AAN process.

This research was sponsored by the Deputy Chief of Staff for Doctrine, TRADOC, and was conducted in RAND Arroyo Center's Strategy and Doctrine Program. The Arroyo Center is a federally funded research and development center sponsored by the United States Army.

CONTENTS

FIGURE

The high-level AAN wargames provide a structured forum for a discussion of national security issues associated with the nature of warfare in the early-to-mid 21st century. Analysis of the game consists of assessing the influence of player positions on issues associated with future warfare. These issues are included in a set of research questions prepared before the game. A complete list of the research questions is included in the appendix.

During the game, TRAC and RAND Arroyo Center analysts produced daily chronologies focusing on major events and decisions taken by the players and assessors. From the discussions leading to these events, issues related to the wargame objectives and research questions were recorded. The analytic teams produced daily summaries of major emerging issues. These summaries were used in producing the Arroyo Center initial impressions report[1] and the TRAC emerging impressions report. Both these reports were submitted to TRADOC and contributed to an initial-impressions memorandum to the CSA.

The Spring Wargame was set in the year 2021. The major game activity involved an attack on the states on the south shore of the Persian Gulf by Red. The United States was also involved in a multinational peacekeeping operation in Indonesia. In addition, continuing border conflict between India and Pakistan escalated dangerously during the game, eventually resulting in nuclear weapon use.

---

[1]Walter L. Perry and Bruce R. Pirnie, *The Army After Next 1998 Spring Wargame: Initial Impressions,* Santa Monica, CA: RAND, PM-809-A, 1998.

These three separate events were designed to examine the role of AAN forces in global conflicts.

Five dominant themes cut across the thirteen issues identified in this study: rapid deployment into theater, asymmetric responses, urban warfare, homeland defense, and information operations. Although space continued to be important, the fact that the enemy had no ability to launch attacks in or from space removed space as a dominating concern in this game.

Asymmetric responses: Red recognized that it could not confront the superior firepower, speed, and situational awareness of the Blue AAN forces and therefore resorted to asymmetric responses. The Red commander executed two tactics designed to prevent the AAN Battle Force[2] from attacking Red forces in the open. These two tactics were to "hide" in the cities and to shield its forces with noncombatants ("hugging"). When the Battle Force arrived, it was thwarted by these tactics and consequently was forced to wait in host nation territory (Egypt and the MOB[3]) for Army XXI forces to arrive. To further post-

---

[2]The three Battle Forces played in SWG 98 were conceptual air-mechanized forces notionally available in 2021. Each Battle Force could self-deploy globally and conduct independent operations. The air-mechanized concept emphasized rapid maneuver in operational depth and quick destruction of opposing heavy forces through concentrations of precise long-range fires. Battle Force commanders would accept limited periods of close combat if necessary, but they normally planned to engage opposing forces at standoff ranges, i.e., beyond ten kilometers. At game start, the three Battle Forces were located as follows: BF-1 at Fort Stewart, Georgia; BF-2 at Fort Hood, Texas; and BF-3 at Fort Lewis, Washington, with some units deployed to Incirlik, Turkey.

Each Battle Force was roughly brigade-sized and included a headquarters, attack aviation unit, a transport aviation unit, a fire support unit, a logistical unit, a reconnaissance unit, and six battle units. The transport aviation unit was equipped with tilt-rotor aircraft capable of lifting 15-ton vehicles. These tilt-rotor aircraft were air-refuelable and had an unrefueled range of approximately 2,000 nautical miles, thus permitting global mobility. The fire support unit was equipped with 15-ton fire support vehicles and fire support pods. These pods could be air-dropped, left unattended, and operated remotely. The reconnaissance unit included a section that operated unmanned aerial vehicles (UAV) and several air reconnaissance sections. The battle units were equipped with 15-ton combat vehicles that carried both direct-fire weapons and non-line-of-sight (NLOS) weapons. The NLOS weapons could deliver precision-guided munitions up to 60 kilometers. These 15-ton combat vehicles featured signature reduction, passive protection against heavy machine gun rounds, and possibly active protection against kinetic energy rounds of larger caliber. Battle units also had reconnaissance sections operating smaller UAV.

[3]The Mobile Offshore Base (MOB) was a conceptual basing option notionally available in 2021. A typical MOB consisted of four towed sections that could be deployed,

pone the arrival of Army XXI forces, Red conducted a wide-ranging information warfare (IW) campaign coupled with attacks on the U.S. homeland. This strategy was aimed at: (1) convincing the U.S. public that reserve component forces were needed at home and (2) disrupting troop staging areas and ports of embarkation.

Urban warfare: Within the five-day window before AAN Battle Forces arrived, Red forces dashed to undefended cities and prepared new defensive positions. The AAN Battle Forces were clearly unsuited for urban operations. Its tilt-rotors and light armored vehicles were very vulnerable to enemy fire coming from concealed locations such as buildings. Also, the precision-guided munitions (PGMs) and information systems of the Battle Force were seriously degraded in the city. Finally, the enemy guessed that the Blue National Command Authority (NCA) would not allow an attack in any situation where there was a strong likelihood that large numbers of innocent civilians would be harmed. Consequently, Blue declined to commit Battle Forces in urban terrain and was compelled to rely on coalition forces or wait for Army XXI units to close in theater. Operations in cities, especially cities in Gulf States allied with Blue, became a central theme of the wargame.

Rapid deployment: The dominant feature of this wargame was *the inability of Blue to deploy a decisive force in a timely manner.* The absence of adequate forward-deployed forces meant that AAN forces had to be deployed from the U.S. homeland. Even under the most optimistic assumptions about self-deployment, en route refueling, and debarkation, the AAN Battle Force took five days to arrive. This gave Red adequate time to plan and execute asymmetric strategies that essentially frustrated the precision-strike capabilities of the AAN Battle Force and the early-arriving airforce units. As a result it was not until much later, when the Army XXI forces arrived, that Blue was prepared to dislodge the enemy. The early-arriving forces were therefore not decisive and the decisive forces arrived late.

---

assembled, and anchored in international waters to provide landing fields for fixed- and rotary-wing aircraft, aircraft maintenance, aviation resupply, medical support, logistical support, and other services. It could support Marine aviation, Navy aviation, or Army aviation, including Army rotary-wing aircraft and conceptual Battle Forces deploying with tilt-rotor aircraft.

Information operations: Anticipating that Blue would enjoy an overwhelming advantage in information operations, Red allowed his commanders considerable autonomy at the lowest practical levels. Red issued detailed pre-war, mission-type orders, thus permitting his commanders to go on "autopilot" and move toward their objectives even when links to the Red NCA were broken. By using this procedure, Red hoped to deny collection opportunities and to reduce the effectiveness of Blue attempts to jam or distort communications. Red also attempted to utilize commercial communications systems that were "below the threshold of Blue's information detection systems" to communicate with and control far-flung Special Operations Forces (SOF) units.

Homeland defense: The Red campaign in the United States consisted of limited attacks against selected ports of embarkation and other military targets. In addition, Red waged an extensive propaganda campaign aimed at convincing the U.S. public that Red aims were simply to free the holy cities for access to all Muslims (including Americans) and to open the Gulf of Islam to all navigation except military vessels. The effect was to slow the deployment of units to the Gulf and raise concerns among the state governors about the federalization of National Guard units.

The following list includes all of the major issues we discerned during the game. All are related to the research questions identified by TRAC prior to the game.[4] The issues are divided into two categories: those that directly affect decisions on the organization, equipment, and training of AAN forces, and those that are of general interest to Army planners.

AAN ISSUES

"Hugging" tactic: How can Army forces operate effectively when an enemy shields its forces with noncombatants?

Urban warfare: What kinds of Army forces would be best able to clear and secure cities without suffering unacceptable casualties?

---

[4] *Analysis Plan for the Army After Next Spring Wargame 1998,* TRAC, March 1998, also see the appendix.

Deployment speed: How can Army forces deploy rapidly enough to achieve a quick decision required by the NCA?

Information operations: How can the Army conduct effective information operations against an enemy who decentralizes command and control?

Coalition warfare: To what extent should Army forces be equipped and trained to operate effectively in coalition with foreign forces?

Post-conflict stability: How might the Army contribute to post-conflict stability?

Battle Force soldiers: How should commissioned and noncommissioned officers (NCOs) be trained to assure they make maximum use of the Battle Force's combat potential?

Reserve and National Guard roles: What are appropriate roles for the Army Reserve and National Guard forces?

OTHER ISSUES

Predelegation of authority: What authority to employ space-based weapons should NCA predelegate to CINCSPACE?

Preventing nuclear use: How could the NCA prevent third countries from using nuclear weapons against each other?

Denying commercial space assets: How could the NCA discourage use of commercial space assets by an enemy while increasing its own capability?

Use of space-based weapons: Under what circumstances should the NCA authorize first use of space-based weapons against terrestrial targets?

Homeland defense: How should civilian and military organizations be organized and controlled to conduct effective defense of the homeland?

RECOMMENDATIONS

1. Develop a spectrum of concepts for the AAN Battle Force.

The Army should develop a spectrum of concepts for the Army After Next Battle Force. Previous wargames tended to demonstrate advantages of the current air-mech concept, while the Spring Wargame tended to demonstrate limitations.

The current air-mech concept has these advantages:

Global self-deployment: In the current concept, air-mech forces deploy with organic tilt-rotor aircraft from their home bases into a theater of operations using combinations of intermediate staging bases and aerial refueling.

Vertical maneuver: Once in theater, air-mech forces use their organic tilt-rotor aircraft for operational and tactical mobility.

Precision fire: Air-mech forces have not only highly effective direct-fire weapons, but also advanced indirect-fire weapons that allow precise engagement at great depths.

The current air-mech concept has these limitations:

Inability to fight in urban terrain: In the Spring Wargame, Red's use of urban terrain largely negated the effectiveness of air-mech Battle Forces.

Inability to hold ground. Air-mech Battle Forces are designed to conduct strike missions, then quickly relocate. They are not designed to seize and hold parts of the earth's surface against opposing forces that are designed for traditional land warfare.

Vulnerability to air defense: The air-mech Battle Force is intended to strike at opposing heavy forces. The Spring Wargame suggested that such opportunities may be limited, in part due to opposing air defense.

Considering these limitations to the air-mech concept, the Army needs to develop and examine other concepts for its future forces. Like the air-mech concept, these concepts should be designed to win campaigns swiftly and decisively with minimal collateral damage.

Among the concepts that might be selected for more detailed study are:

Air/sea-lifted light armor force: Combat vehicles weighing 20–30 tons might have enough protection to accept close engagement in constrictive terrain.

Sea-lifted medium armor force: Combat vehicles weighing 30–40 tons (roughly half the current weight) might have enough protection to assure successful engagement in constrictive terrain and also dismount significantly greater numbers of infantry.

2. Study deployment and logistics support.

During the Spring Wargame, deployment and logistics received more attention than they did in previous wargames, but much work remains to be done. The Army needs to study these issues for the current air-mech concept and for other concepts as well. There may be little point in examining the operational utility of forces that could not deploy strategically or be sustained in theater as assumed.

3. Explore ways to cooperate with allies.

It is axiomatic that the United States will not fight alone. According to *Army Vision 2010:* "Land component operations in 2010 will be fully integrated with those of joint, multinational, and nongovernmental partners. Recent experience reminds us that Army operations have never been and never will be independent."

During the Spring Wargame, allied contributions were critical, including those of regional allies and of NATO partners. Without allied contributions, the Gulf States would have been overwhelmed before Blue could even halt Red forces, much less strike a decisive blow. Therefore it is important to understand how Army forces, especially conceptual forces developed in Army After Next, would operate in conjunction with allied forces despite dissimilarities in weapons and doctrine. There may also be circumstances in which an opponent would fight in coalition.

The authors are grateful for the guidance and assistance of several analysts at TRAC and TRADOC. We especially acknowledge the assistance provided by COL Steve Kirin, Director of TRAC at Fort Leavenworth. Colonel Kirin served as the head of the Spring Wargame analysis team and in that capacity directed the joint TRAC/Arroyo Center analytic effort. His comments and suggestions were very helpful in preparing this report. During the game, Peggy Fratzel and Mike Ingram kept the Arroyo Center and TRAC teams informed of the operational issues being developed by the TRAC analysis team. LTC Henry G. Franke III, TRADOC, assisted in the preparation of the technology assessments. The tasks of collecting information from the various player and assessment cells and developing the wargame issues were shared by the Arroyo Center and TRAC. The nine Arroyo Center analysts were Richard Darilek, Scot Eisenhard, LTC Robert Everson, Matt Gershwin, John Gordon, Tom Herbert, Bob Howe, Maren Leed, and Lt. Col. Gail Wojtowicz. Most have considerable experience in gaming, simulations, and exercises. The authors also wish to thank Dave Kassing for volunteering his time to assist in the data-collection effort. Finally, we are grateful for the thoughtful comments and suggestions provided by our two reviewers, Paul Davis and Colonel (ret.) Rick Sinnereich.

Theme	A unifying concept.
Issue	A controversy for which there are two or more positions. We attempt to *resolve* issues.
Objective	A desired outcome of a process. We try to *achieve* objectives.
Research question	A problem that can be solved using the tools of analysis. We *answer* research questions.

Chapter One

INTRODUCTION

The high-level Army After Next (AAN) wargames are designed to provide a structured forum for a discussion of national security issues associated with the nature of warfare in the early-to-mid 21st century. Inputs to the games consist of postulated 2021 force structures for Red, Blue, and other countries, and a scenario that includes a "history of the future." Analysis of the game consists of assessing the influence of player positions on issues associated with future warfare. These issues are included in a set of research questions prepared prior to the game.[1] The results are not expected to produce definitive conclusions about the nature of future warfare, or about the structure of the future AAN force; rather, they inform the development and refinement of research issues for follow-on analysis.

CONNECTING TO THE R&D PROCESS

One of the AAN requirements set by Army Chief of Staff is "to ensure that the [long-term vision of the Army] connects . . . to the Army's research and development (R&D) programs."[2] This connection is important given the lead time historically required to develop new weapon systems. The R&D community has been invited to participate in both the planning for and execution of the AAN wargames. The latter participation has generally been through the Technology Special Team that meets continuously during the game to discuss the technological implications of the required future force capabilities.

---

[1] A complete list of these questions is included in the appendix.

[2] *Army After Next Spring Wargame Game Book*, TRADOC, p. 35, April 1998.

New technologies often imply new operational art and tactics. Conversely, the desire for new combat capabilities can lead to a search for new technologies. For example, vastly improved sensing and information processing offers the commander superior target acquisition capability and situational awareness. The former enhances the future forces' ability to deliver precision munitions at greater stand-off distances, whereas the latter improves the commander's ability to maneuver his force intelligently.

In this report we focus on the issues from the game that have the greatest implications for new or improved technologies and/or operational procedures. The list of issues is by no means exhaustive. Several other important issues and insights were gained from the game and are reported elsewhere.[3]

ORGANIZATION OF THIS REPORT

The next two chapters provide context for the discussion of the issues that ensue. Chapter Two describes the game methodology, and Chapter Three provides an overview of the game events. The next two chapters present the issues arising from game play. Chapter Four focuses on issues that directly affect the design and operation of future Army forces, and Chapter Five discusses game issues that are associated with warfare in the 2021 timeframe but do not affect the AAN directly. In both chapters, the issue is identified and discussed within the context of the game. The decisions taken by the players to resolve the issue (if any) are presented next, followed by further suggestions for resolving the issue or for conducting further research to do so. Each issue ends with an assessment of its technological and operational implications. In Chapter Six we conclude with recommendations to improve the AAN process.

------

[3]See *The Army After Next 1998 Spring Wargame Emerging Impressions Report,* TRAC, May 1998.

Chapter Two

METHODOLOGY

The methodology used in the 1998 Spring Wargame (SWG) is a refinement of the AAN wargame methodology first used in the Winter Wargame in 1997. Since then, the process and procedures have been revised to increase efficiency and to improve the utility of game results.

GAME STRUCTURE

The SWG consisted of two connected two-sided games, Red versus Blue and Orange versus Blue. Orange represented the New Nationalist Movement (NNM), a Transnational Criminal Organization (TCO) that had established a de facto state in northern Sumatra. In addition, a separate India-Pakistan conflict was played within the game.[1] The game consisted of two events separated by approximately one month. The first was a political-military workshop designed to establish the national objectives of both Red and Blue, and to set the conditions for the beginning of hostilities.[2] The second event was the two-week game in April at the Center for Strategic Leadership,

---

[1] The India-Pakistan conflict was played as a separate game within a game with self-adjudication. The events in this game and the adjudicated results were reconciled with the larger game by the game assessors during the nightly adjudication process.

[2] The workshop goals outlined in the workshop game book are to "set Blue and Red national policies, strategies, conditions and guidance relative to the situation that initiates war in the April game" and to "determine the key events, actions, and reactions that would have been taken or would have occurred prior to war." See *Army After Next 1998 Spring Wargame Political-Military Workshop Game Book*, TRADOC, March 1998.

Carlisle Barracks, Pennsylvania, that focused primarily on prosecuting the war. Figure 2.1 illustrates the game structure and the interaction of these two events. The wargame itself consisted of five game turns, each of varying real-time duration. The state of play at the beginning of each turn was the state of play at the end of the previous game turn plus Control inputs. Of the many gaming attributes, those discussed below are of particular importance to the Spring Wargame.

Inputs

The inputs to the political-military workshop consisted of a "State of the World from 1998 to 2021," with an emphasis on events in the Middle East and in South Asia. These inputs were generally referred to as the *history of the future*. The players received additional information about information operations, Blue space policy, international space agreements, Reserve Component policy, and logistics. Blue and Red "After Next" forces were also briefed, but because the main focus of the workshop was political, little detail about these forces was provided.

The national strategies for both Red and Blue resulting from the workshop along with the "conditions and guidance relative to the

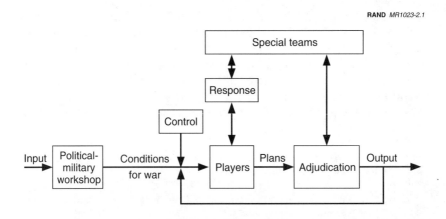

Figure 2.1—Spring Wargame Structure

situation that initiates war"[3] were used by Control to develop a situation at the start of the Carlisle Barracks game that would lead directly to war. In addition to the threatening situation confronting both teams, the players were given the postulated force structures for both Blue and Red forces along with operational concepts for each.

Players

At each game turn, processing began with the force status resulting from the adjudication from the previous game turn. Control on occasion interjected direction either through the adjudication process or directly through the players. During the plan development process, several interactions took place among opposing sides, among the sides and allies or neutrals, and between the sides and international bodies such as the United Nations (UN), The North Atlantic Treaty Organization (NATO), etc. In addition, specific information about aspects of the 2021 world not found in the resource material was available from the Response cell. This aspect of the game was especially important with respect to technical information on specialized functions such as information operations, space, and logistics. Once plans were formulated on both sides, they were forwarded to the assessment teams for adjudication.

Adjudication

Players generated plans that were transmitted to the assessment teams for adjudication. Ideally, the adjudication process consists of the *consistent application of well-documented rules.* This occurs naturally in computer simulations of combat through the application of decision rules that, although never complete, nevertheless guarantee consistency. In wargames such as the SWG, decision rules constitute only a portion of the adjudication process. A large component of adjudication consists of subjective assessments by experts, so consistent application of rules becomes more problematic. In its place, assessment teams seek *reasonable outcomes.*

---

[3]See *AAN 1998 Spring Wargame Political Military Workshop: Workshop Guide,* TRADOC, 22–24 March, 1998.

The major sources of decision rules are the annual *tactical wargames*, the *franchise games,* and TRADOC-sponsored *workshops.* Each of these is described below.

- **Tactical wargames:** These are held annually at TRAC Fort Leavenworth and are designed to capture the tactical effects of the postulated Red and Blue 2021 forces. Usually, three scenarios are proposed with two or three vignettes examined for each scenario. Players consist of former and currently serving military officers from all services as well as defense agency representatives and defense contractors. The results of the games are added to the results from previous tactical wargames to enlarge the decision rule set.

- **Franchise games:** TRADOC has granted franchises to several organizations to investigate how likely future advances in special combat and combat-related areas will affect warfare in the 2021 timeframe. To date, TRADOC has granted franchises in the following areas: sustainment and logistics, special operations, information operations, and space operations. In the past year, several small wargames focusing on each of these areas were conducted. The results of these exercises contributed to rule sets and enhanced scenarios that were used in the SWG.

- **Workshops:** In addition to the franchise games, several workshops were conducted throughout the year to examine special areas of interest. Some of these include "graybeard" workshops to examine issues in information operations, deployment and logistics, and space operations. The results of these activities also contributed to the rule sets for their special fields.

During game play, the functions of adjudication, play, and control were kept strictly separate to avoid blurring cause-and-effect relationships. The Response Team was added to the game structure to act as a buffer between the players and the Special Teams located with the assessors. The major player cells were assigned experts in special areas, e.g., a Commander in Chief, Space (CINCSPACE) was added to the Blue staff. These experts were used to offer advice and to direct operations in their field of expertise. However, technical questions requiring answers from the supporting Special Teams were funneled through the Response Team in order to maintain clear separation. Issuing door passes to the players that admitted them only into their own cells enforced physical separation.

Special Teams

There are several aspects of future warfare that cut across organizational structures and operational concepts. These include information operations (IO), space and missile defense, deployment, sustainment and logistics, and weapons of mass destruction (WMD). Although it was clear that these activities needed to be represented in the AAN wargames, before the first AAN wargame in January 1997 it was not clear how they might interact with each other and with the After Next forces. Consequently, these activities were represented in Special Teams and were available to advise either side at all levels of play and the assessors as well.

In the SWG, thanks to the franchise games and the two previous AAN wargames, a clearer view of the role of the Special Teams has emerged, and the experts are more fully integrated with the players and assessors. However, the Special Teams remain to provide additional expertise as required through the Response Team buffer.

Free Play

A free play game can be risky because game play may not move in appropriate directions. For example, players may wish to avoid war and resort to diplomatic negotiations, precluding the examination of issues associated with future combat.

To minimize interference in a free play game, game planners used the political-military workshop to establish a "road to war." The workshop produced conditions for war, and the Game Directors developed a scenario consistent with these conditions so that war was imminent at the start of the game. The Game Directors also exercised some direction through the adjudication process and through interventions with the players. The players were aware of these interventions and generally accepted them as necessary to achieve game objectives. Within these bounds, the players were free to take any decisions they chose. The objective was to allow the players to act out their roles in the context of the scenario and thereby raise important issues. Planners recognized that too many interventions by the Game Directors might repress the free flow of ideas by focusing the participants too narrowly and might therefore reduce the number of issues addressed.

Analysis

TRAC Fort Leavenworth led the analysis effort for the SWG. The Arroyo Center assigned analysts to eight team cells to observe game play and the adjudication process. Both a TRAC and an Arroyo Center analyst were assigned to several of the more important team cells. Each analyst produced a daily chronology of events with emphasis on the decisions taken by the players and assessors. In cells to which both an Arroyo Center and a TRAC analyst were posted, a single chronology was submitted. In addition to the chronology, each analyst was asked to indicate how the events observed informed one or more of the 18 issues of interest to TRADOC (see the appendix). These reports were submitted daily and a set of emerging impressions was prepared daily for the Game Director's meeting.

In addition to the reports on the special issues, several of the observer/analysts (including three from the Arroyo Center) were designated "lead analyst" for one or more of the issues. These individuals were responsible for gathering all information concerning the issues they were assigned in preparation for producing separate reports on each. These reports will be used by TRAC to produce the final game report.

At the last meeting of the player teams, a questionnaire was distributed to all players. They were asked to comment on 2 of the 18 issues from their perspective and role in the game. These reports were made available to both the Arroyo Center and TRAC analysts for inclusion in the final reports.

Chapter Three

GAME OVERVIEW

The 1998 Army After Next Spring Wargame (SWG) was set in the year 2021. The major game activity involved an attack on the states on the south shore of the Persian Gulf by Red. The United States was also involved in a multinational peacekeeping operation in Indonesia. A continuing border conflict between India and Pakistan escalated dangerously during the game, eventually resulting in nuclear weapon use. Some individual European countries supported the U.S. actions aimed at preventing nuclear escalation.

NATO was not initially involved as an organization in the conflict with Red. This changed during the course of the game after Turkey was attacked and Article 5 response brought NATO as a whole into the conflict. Russia and China were neutral but resented U.S. actions to deny its enemies the use of commercial satellites. Russia, for example, provided Red with satellite information on U.S. assets in the Gulf.

Although the strategic context of the scenario was established in advance, player teams represented countries expected to make decisions in the game. The game was conducted in five moves that covered a simulated time of about 45 days.

Commanders of the U.S. forces in the Middle East initially contemplated very sweeping attacks into the heartland of the aggressor nation. However, limitations on deployment and the necessity to reopen the Persian Gulf confined all U.S. and coalition force operations to the vicinity of the Persian Gulf until relatively late in the game. As the game ended, coalition forces had largely cleared the west shore of the Persian Gulf of enemy forces and were moving north.

A key aspect of the game was the decision by Red to enter poorly defended urban areas and keep its forces there once the cities had been seized. As a result, the most modernized U.S. units, which were specifically designed to exploit the effects of long-range precision fires through operational maneuver, had little utility, and the urban areas had to be cleared by coalition forces, U.S. Marine Corps units, and Army XXI units. This enemy move proved to be an effective asymmetric counter to significant U.S. technological superiority.

Chapter Four

ARMY AFTER NEXT ISSUES

The following issues could directly affect decisions on the organization, equipment, and training of AAN forces. We relate each issue to
the research questions[1] set by TRADOC, DCSDOC for the 1998 SWG,
explain how each issue emerged from game play, briefly explore
possible resolutions, and suggest technological and operational implications.

HOW CAN ARMY FORCES OPERATE EFFECTIVELY WHEN AN ENEMY SHIELDS HIS FORCES WITH NONCOMBATANTS?[2]

Shielding forces in this way was called "hugging" during the game.
This tactic was used because Red believed that Blue would not attack
an enemy military formation if there were danger that innocent
civilians could be harmed.

Game Play

During the game, Red and Orange both engaged in "hugging" tactics:
Red proclaimed a "Haj (pilgrimage) of the Dispossessed," while
Orange staged a "Reunification March." Blue and Saudi Arabia

---

[1]A complete list of the 18 research questions is in *Analysis Plan for the Army After Next Spring Wargame 1998*, TRADOC Analysis Center, 8 April 1998, and in the appendix.

[2]Research Question 14, Asymmetries: What are the potential vulnerabilities of AAN forces to asymmetric counters? What asymmetric counters might future adversaries pursue, as demonstrated in this conflict?

feared that the "pilgrimage" would provide cover to Red operatives and possibly Red military forces. But shortly after it began, Red transitioned to a conventional invasion of Saudi Arabia, obviating a need for Blue or allied forces to deal with this "Haj."

Red also expected that large numbers of civilians inside captured Saudi cities would help to shield Red forces from Blue attack.

Red seized oil company personnel and transported them to key Red facilities. The presence of these civilians would be announced and the "interned" civilians would be released very slowly. In addition, Red intercepted ships in the Persian Gulf and escorted them to Red ports in order to inhibit strikes by Blue.

Orange proclaimed a "Reunification March" of civilians from northern Sumatra through the zone of separation into Indonesia. Brown (the government of Indonesia) feared that Orange would use this march to infiltrate agents and special operations forces. Blue assisted Brown in frustrating the march and Orange eventually ceased its sponsorship, causing the marchers to return home. Orange subsequently proclaimed a second march but fewer people were willing to participate due to the previous fiasco.

Neither the Battle Forces nor Army XXI forces were prepared to handle mass movements of civilians that might contain enemy operatives or shield the advance of military forces. For humanitarian and political reasons, the Blue NCA did not authorize the employment of lethal force in circumstances that would have entailed heavy losses of noncombatants.

During game play, Blue expected Saudi forces to counter the "Haj of the Dispossessed" from Iraq into Saudi Arabia. In contrast, Blue persuaded Brown not to directly confront the Orange-sponsored "Reunification March." Instead, Blue and allied contingents used nonlethal means to discourage marchers and helped to interdict seaborne traffic with naval forces. Brown used information operations (false Web sites, radio and television broadcasts) to turn back the marchers.

Possible resolutions:[3] U.S. adversaries have employed several variations of the "hugging" tactic. In Iraq, in 1991, Saddam Hussein intermingled civilians and military assets to discourage U.S. bombing. In Somalia, in 1993, Mohammed Farah Aideed's militia deliberately used women and children to shield their actions. The United States may have to enlist the help of regional allies to counter "hugging" tactics. But even with their help, this tactic may be difficult to counter.

Technological Implications

The United States and its allies might employ nonlethal weapons to strip civilian cover from military operations or to disrupt mass movements of civilians that run counter to U.S. interests. These means might include agents that inhibited movement, such as sticky substances and foam, and psychological means. But for political and humanitarian reasons, the United States might be extremely reluctant to employ nonlethal weapons that cause severe symptoms or altered mental states. The United States might also employ information operations to disrupt the organization and support of mass civilian movements. Precision munitions could cripple the transportation infrastructure required to support mass movements without causing large civilian casualties.

Operational Implications

The United States will usually prefer whenever possible to have allied forces deal with the problem of "hugging." Allies may be more willing to assume responsibility for civilian casualties, either accidental or intentional, that may occur during the operation. Their forces may be better able to distinguish innocent civilians from enemy operatives in cases where they are intermingled.

---

[3]In discussion of possible resolutions, technological implications, and operational implications, we assume that Blue experience is valid for the United States.

WHAT KINDS OF ARMY FORCES WOULD BE BEST ABLE TO CLEAR AND SECURE CITIES WITHOUT SUFFERING UNACCEPTABLE CASUALTIES?[4]

Game Play

Operations in cities, especially cities in Gulf States allied with Blue, were a central issue of the 1998 SWG. Anticipating that Blue Battle Forces would enjoy overwhelming superiority in open terrain, Red dashed for weakly defended key cities in Gulf States and prepared to defend them from a Blue counterattack. Blue declined to enter these cities with Battle Forces because they were considered unsuited for urban combat.

The Blue President and his military advisors sought ways to avoid urban combat. They considered bypassing cities, cutting Red lines of communication, and starving Red forces out. These tactics were unacceptable because Blue coalition partners and Blue domestic opinion demanded quicker results. The Blue President feared that support for the war, home and abroad, would decline if operations became too protracted. Coalition partners considered protracted sieges unacceptable because their own civilians would be the first to starve. Ultimately, Blue forces would fail in their mission unless they could compel timely removal of Red forces and destroy their combat power.

The Blue President initially expected that Battle Forces would have at least some effectiveness in urban areas. But his military advisors strongly counseled against sending Battle Forces into built-up terrain where they could not use long-range precision fires directly and would be vulnerable to enemy forces fighting at close range. They explained that the Battle Force was equipped with vehicles that were too small to carry sufficient infantry and too thin-skinned to risk close combat.

---

[4]Research Question 8, Urban Operations: What operational concepts should be used during the employment of AAN-era Battle Forces in large urban areas? What are the critical limitations and vulnerabilities associated with the employment of AAN-era Battle Forces in large urban areas? What roles did coalition forces or civil authorities play?

Based on this advice, the Blue President relied on coalition forces and Marine forces until Army XXI forces arrived in theater. Coalition forces, especially German light forces and Saudi National Guard heavy forces, were successful, but suffered heavy casualties. The Blue II Marine Expeditionary Force (MEF) suffered heavy casualties when it entered built-up terrain in the Basra area and engaged a corps-sized concentration of Red 2020 units. (A Marine advisor stated that given Blue intelligence capabilities, Blue commanders would have recognized that this operation would entail unacceptably high losses and therefore would have found another way to handle Red forces in the vicinity of Basra. Ironically, Blue III Corps, a force with sufficient land power to conduct the operation, passed north of Basra on its way into the Red homeland a few days later.) The Blue President was shocked by these casualty figures. He felt that the American people would not accept such losses in a war that did not appear to involve a vital national interest.

Red's urban operations had two major components. First, Red lunged for key Saudi and Gulf State cities. Red forces advanced by land and through air assault. Once taken, these cities were prepared for 360-degree defense. Second, Red created fortified "hedgehogs" inside its homeland. Certain cities received entire corps for their defense. When reserves were mobilized (including 20 reserve divisions) they were immediately deployed into other, smaller, Red cities to increase the "web" of fortified locations. Red's most successful use of this strategy was in Riyadh and Basra. In both locations Blue and/or Blue coalition forces engaged in intense urban combat to eject Red. Heavy losses resulted in both instances. Red's leadership remarked, "What would happen if Blue had to do 25 Riyadhs?" Red hoped that as Blue forces extended their advance into the Red homeland, more urban engagements would result. Red regarded this network of defended cities as its main means to defend its homeland against Blue ground attack.

Blue players considered several possible solutions to the problem of combat in urban areas:

- Create urban warfare modules in Battle Forces.
- Support coalition forces fighting in urban areas.

- Use Marine forces.

- Wait for Army XXI forces to arrive.

Game players considered providing modules specialized in urban combat that could be attached to Battle Forces. However, they recognized that these modules could delay deployment and might be incompatible with the faster-moving Battle Forces. During game play, Blue generally chose the second option because German forces, British forces, Saudi forces, and other Gulf State forces were available. It supported these coalition forces with land-based aviation, carrier-based aviation, naval gunfire, and limited Battle Force operations. As heavy Blue forces became available they also took part. Blue also used Marine forces extensively in built-up areas, including the United Arab Emirates (UAE), the vicinity of Bandar Abbas, and Basra. The Marines were successful everywhere, but suffered heavy casualties in Basra as noted. Blue waited until several Army XXI divisions were near closure before initiating deep land operations in the Red homeland where additional Red 2020 divisions were prepared for defense in bastion-like urban terrain.

Possible resolutions: Army XXI forces will probably have to perform urban combat in the 2020 timeframe. As currently configured, Battle Forces could not perform this combat effectively. If Battle Forces were reconfigured to conduct urban combat, they would very likely forfeit agility, making their "fire ambush" tactic infeasible.

Technological Implications

An air-mechanized Battle Force could operate successfully in urban terrain if its vehicles offered sufficient protection and could transport sufficient infantry, but these features appear unobtainable within a conceptual 15-ton weight limit. Marine and Army XXI units operating in urban terrain will need nonlethal weapons with area effects, sophisticated sensors (including sensors using nanotechnology), extremely accurate positioning, armored protection, robotic air and ground vehicles, and more comprehensive personal protection for the soldier.

Operational Implications

Allied countries could be encouraged to take measures to secure the land approaches to their cities with strong defenses and also prepare to prevent air assault. But if opposing forces reached friendly cities where they could "go to ground," U.S. forces might still have to defeat them in urban terrain, as occurred at the end of the 1998 SWG. For this reason, Army forces will have to maintain and improve proficiency to conduct urban combat in joint and combined operations, optimally including early-entry forces.

HOW CAN ARMY FORCES DEPLOY RAPIDLY ENOUGH TO ACHIEVE A QUICK DECISION REQUIRED BY THE NCA?[5]

Game Play

The Blue President was dissatisfied with the arrival times of Army forces. In a previous AAN game, he had observed Battle Forces deploying to remote locations in two days. As a result, the more realistic five days assessed during the 1998 SWG seemed slow. Moreover, Battle Forces were unable to accomplish major goals, especially the elimination of Red's offensive combat power, because Red forces had "gone to ground" in urban areas. Therefore, Commander in Chief, Western Command (CINCWEST)[6] had to wait for the arrival of Army XXI forces to conduct decisive operations. The Blue President felt that this delay, approximately two months from the onset of hostilities, was too long because he was under heavy international and domestic pressure to achieve his goals and to conclude the war quickly. In fact, at the end of game play, international opinion had begun to favor acceptance of a cease-fire on Red's terms.

Red was very much influenced by Blue's rapid deployment capability. Red's plan depended on "going to ground" in undefended Saudi urban areas before Blue forces arrived in theater. At the same time,

---

[5]Research Question 6, Pace: Given greater emphasis on speed, mobility, and information, what is the impact of the pace of warfare on decision making in 2021? What actions did Red/Orange use to influence Blue's pace?

[6]In this game, CINCWEST was responsible for operations west of the Pakistan-Iran border and CINCEAST was responsible for operations east of the border.

Red intended to attack Blue's deployment capability, both in the Blue homeland and in theater using lethal and nonlethal means.

A Battle Force stationed in Korea deployed to the Persian Gulf and was replaced by the Blue 38th Infantry Division from CONUS. CINCEAST was concerned that withdrawal of the highly capable Battle Force, although replaced by a larger force, might suggest to Korea and China that the United States placed lower priority on Northeast Asia. Forward stationing may reduce deployment time for Battle Forces, but it may also inhibit their use in other theaters.

At the same time, the Blue 10th Mountain Division deployed from CONUS to Guam, a central location in CINCEAST's area of responsibility. But when conflict began in the Persian Gulf, CINCEAST was no longer allocated sufficient lift assets to move the division readily. In retrospect, CINCEAST should have deployed this division to some threatened area or left it in CONUS.

Possible resolutions: In their current configuration, Battle Forces cannot accomplish all the missions required for rapid conflict termination. Therefore, more rapid or larger-scale deployment of Battle Forces would not resolve this issue. With limited U.S. support, coalition forces might be strong enough to achieve decisive success, but more likely Army XXI forces will be required. Therefore, the challenge is to deploy these forces more rapidly.

Technological Implications

Army XXI forces might use more maritime prepositioning or forward deployment in peacetime to speed their arrival. Ultrafast sealift would help resolve the issue. Such sealift might first appear as commercial ventures and subsequently find military application. The Army could also develop forces that are lighter than the current heavy force yet still able to accomplish fundamental land force missions, for example, securing key terrain and compelling the surrender of opposing land forces, wherever they choose to hide or entrench themselves. A combination of ultrafast sealift and lighter Army forces could be the most promising approach to resolving this issue. The United States may also have to develop "ultrafast escort ships" to protect the faster sealift.

Operational Implications

As currently configured, Battle Forces may often be unable to achieve decisive success without help from Army XXI forces. In some situations, allied forces might be critically important during the first phase of a campaign. Therefore, these highly disparate forces must train together and, to the extent possible, deploy within mutually supporting distances.

HOW CAN THE ARMY CONDUCT EFFECTIVE INFORMATION OPERATIONS AGAINST AN ENEMY WHO DECENTRALIZES COMMAND AND CONTROL?[7]

Game Play

Anticipating that Blue would intercept or jam communications, Red decided to allow its commanders considerable autonomy at the lowest practical levels, i.e., corps, division, and separate brigade maneuver forces. Red issued detailed pre-war, mission-type orders to its major commands, thus permitting them to go on "autopilot" and move toward their objectives even when constant links to the Red NCA might not be possible. By using this tactic, Red hoped to deny collection opportunities and to reduce the effectiveness of Blue attempts to deny or distort communications.

In the CINCEAST area of responsibility, Blue conducted information operations against Orange, while Orange conducted information operations against Blue and Brown. Some players expected that information operations, especially Blue's attacks on Orange financial assets, would escalate to armed conflict, but both sides retaliated in kind. Orange was an extremely difficult target because its organization was flat and decentralized. Moreover, it used legitimate businesses to disguise its operations.

---

[7]Research Question 3, Information Operations: How do we integrate the range of information operations into the campaign? To what extent did Blue achieve information dominance at any point in any conflict, throughout the world or in localized areas?

Possible resolutions: The United States could respond to this tactic by decentralizing its own information operations and concentrating on smaller increments of opposing forces. It might also concentrate on disrupting functional areas, such as air defense networks and logistical support.

Technological Implications

To counter this tactic, the United States needs to develop systems that provide usable intelligence of exceptional granularity at lower echelons, potentially at unit level. In addition, the United States may be able to mislead opposing commanders who are out of touch with their higher headquarters.

Operational Implications

Army forces might be able to exploit this tactic to their own advantage. They might exploit the dispersion and lack of connectivity among independently operating Blue forces by creating unforeseen situations for the Red forces. Further, Blue could exploit Red's difficulties in providing logistics support to dispersed units by capitalizing on their lack of mutual support.

TO WHAT EXTENT SHOULD ARMY FORCES BE EQUIPPED AND TRAINED TO OPERATE EFFECTIVELY IN COALITION WITH FOREIGN FORCES?[8]

Game Play

The game highlighted the importance of combined operations in both the Gulf region and Indonesia.

Blue depended on coalition forces, both regional and NATO, to conduct vitally important operations during the opening phase of its

---

[8]Research Question 5, Interoperability: What essential characteristics and capabilities must AAN forces have to ensure interoperability with joint, combined, or allied forces in 2021? When and where did interoperability become critical? What interoperability problems occurred or were raised?

campaign in the Persian Gulf. Coalition forces conducted most of the land operations that regained Riyadh and Dhahran. They played an important role in operations to clear and control the Strait of Hormuz. Particularly important were the German brigades that cleared urban areas of Red forces with the help of Gulf land forces and Blue air forces.

Blue depended on Brown to secure its own territory against Orange threats and to contribute to the anti-piracy campaign. Blue limited its support to Brown because it wished to discourage Brown from launching an offensive campaign in Sumatra while the Gulf conflict was still in progress. However, Blue maintained close contact with Brown forces through its own special operations forces, and Blue supported Brown deployment on one occasion.

On the last day of game play, the Blue Secretary of State said that in his opinion coalition operations were absolutely essential to Blue success. For military and political reasons, Blue would continue to operate with coalition forces. Militarily, Blue needed coalition help to control civilian populations, clear urban areas, provide combat power during the critical first phase of a campaign, and secure territory after conflict had been terminated. Politically, Blue needed coalitions to demonstrate solidarity, both to the international community and to the Blue public.

Possible resolutions: Army special operations forces will probably continue to operate closely with allied and friendly forces during normal peacetime. The demand for their regional expertise is likely to increase as U.S. forces become increasingly based in the continental United States. Army XXI forces must also be prepared to conduct combined operations.

AAN Battle Forces are most effective when operating as part of a combined operation. As early-deploying forces, Battle Forces may have to operate for some period, perhaps weeks, as the only substantial U.S. combat force in the region. During this time, they will be more effective if their operations are at least coordinated with those of regional allies. To achieve this coordination, coalition commanders would need to understand the capabilities of Battle Forces, just as Battle Force commanders would have to understand the capabilities of coalition forces. In addition, the United States and its allies would have to prepare control mechanisms that could be activated during a crisis.

Technological Implications

U.S. forces, including Battle Forces, need interoperability with potential coalition partners, implying communications links, mutual familiarity, common procedures, and at least some experience in combined operations. To some extent, interoperability can be fostered through advanced simulations that put U.S. and foreign forces into a shared virtual environment. As C4ISR[9] systems are developed and fielded, there should be connectivity to key regional allies.

Operational Implications

Forward positioning, frequent combined training exercises, increased foreign military sales, etc., will be required to assure interoperability or at least collaboration during crisis and war. U.S. units deploying for the first time from the United States into a region are likely to be less effective in combined operations than units that have at least some exercise experience. These same principles apply to Battle Forces as well as Army XXI forces.

Some coalition forces will be unable to operate at a pace consistent with U.S. forces, especially future forces that now exist only conceptually. However, a properly equipped and trained combined headquarters might be able to harmonize the operations of these highly disparate forces. In addition, all coalition nations could be encouraged to defend their cities.

---

[9]Command, Control, Communications, Computers, Intelligence, Surveillance, and Reconnaissance.

HOW MIGHT THE ARMY CONTRIBUTE TO POST-CONFLICT STABILITY?[10]

Game Play

In the CINCWEST area of responsibility, game play ended before the conflict had terminated. At game's end, Blue forces were advancing into Red territory. Red forces still held defensive positions in urban areas on the southern littoral of the Gulf while other Red forces were located in major Red cities. The Blue President declined to negotiate an end to the conflict until Blue forces had gained a decisive victory that would allow him to attain his war aims, including the elimination of Red's offensive capability. Nevertheless, Blue players began to express their preliminary thoughts on residual forces.

The Blue President was reluctant to leave large forces in the Gulf region after the conflict. He refused to make Iraqi independence a Blue war aim, as demanded by Saudi Arabia, in part because he believed that this goal would require protracted military engagement. In general, he wanted to return Blue forces to the Blue homeland or to their previous locations as soon as possible after termination of the conflict. He particularly wanted to avoid occupying Red territory. The Blue President initially favored a regional arms control regime, but by game's end he had discarded this idea, in part because he thought that arms control would demand protracted military commitment to enforce the provisions.

The Blue Secretary of State had a different perspective. He foresaw that the post-conflict phase would require extensive negotiations with Red and consultations with allies and other powers, including Russia. He believed that a strong negotiating position required protracted deployment of Blue forces in the region. Moreover, he saw Blue forces as fundamental to continued Blue leadership of the anti-Red coalition. As a result, the Secretary of State asked the President to consider revising his position on residual forces.

---

[10]Research Question 2, Stability Operations: How do end state conditions affect the commitment of residual forces to maintain regional stability? What was the composition and mission of residual forces? What considerations drove this composition? What was the enemy capability to resume hostilities?

In fact, Red had initiated plans to conduct guerrilla warfare against Blue, particularly inside Red homeland areas that Blue might occupy. Red also planned to use SOF to lead guerrilla activities among disaffected groups in Saudi Arabia that Blue and/or coalition forces might retake.

Blue policy toward Indonesia was self-contradictory. Blue sponsored and led a peace operation that implied impartiality between Orange and Brown. But at the same time, Blue supported Brown to some extent in its struggle against Orange, implying that Blue had taken sides.

Some U.S. forces, together with regional forces, were interposed as peacekeepers (Chapter VI) between Orange and Brown. At U.S. instigation, the mission of these forces became peace enforcement (Chapter VII).[11] Korea refused to accept the implied obligation to conduct combat operations against Indonesians and withdrew its brigade, despite strong political pressure from Blue.

Possible resolutions: In the Persian Gulf, the United States might resolve this issue by removing its forces and maintaining an "over the horizon" presence in the region, ready to deploy large forces again on short notice. Alternatively, the United States might leave large forces in the region for a protracted period, perhaps years. If U.S. forces had to occupy former enemy territory for an appreciable time, they might have to contend with terrorist attacks and even irregular warfare. In Indonesia, the United States might resolve this issue by deciding either to remain impartial or to take sides with that party whose interests were most compatible with its own.

Technological Implications

If the United States chose an "over the horizon" approach, then rapid deployment would have been important. The United States might have used maritime prepositioning or a mobile operating base

---

[11]Chapter VI refers to "Pacific Settlement of Disputes"; Chapter VII refers to "Action with Respect to Threats to the Peace, Breaches of the Peace, and Acts of Aggression." From the Charter of the United Nations, San Francisco, June 26, 1945.

(MOB)[12] to support this deployment. Post-conflict forces would have to deter renewed aggression and perhaps also control key terrain. They might also have to control potentially hostile populations and counter nonconventional forces.

Operational Implications

Operationally, the United States might have chosen to conduct recurring large-scale exercises with its Gulf State allies.

HOW SHOULD COMMISSIONED AND NONCOMMISSIONED OFFICERS BE TRAINED AND ASSIGNED TO ASSURE THEY MAKE MAXIMUM USE OF THE BATTLE FORCE'S COMBAT POTENTIAL?[13]

Game Play

The Blue President observed that soldiers in the Battle Force would have to maintain an extremely high level of training. They would have to be constantly ready at short notice to deploy practically anywhere in the world and almost immediately conduct intense combat operations. They would have to conduct combined arms at very low levels, requiring proficiency in an unusually broad spectrum of skills. He wondered how soldiers could meet this very high training requirement.

In addition, soldiers in the Battle Force would have to exercise initiative and independent judgment at lower echelons than currently.

---

[12]The MOB was a conceptual basing option notionally available in 2021. A typical MOB consisted of four towed sections that could be deployed, assembled, and anchored in international waters to provide landing fields for fixed- and rotary-wing aircraft, aircraft maintenance, aviation resupply, medical support, logistics support, and other services. It could support Marine aviation, Navy aviation, or Army aviation, including Army rotary-wing aircraft and conceptual Battle Forces deploying with tilt-rotor aircraft.

[13]Research Question 10, AAN Concepts: What operational concepts and inherent capabilities prove most useful in combating major competitors in 2021? What physical and mental abilities, different from those required today, might be needed by AAN soldiers to execute those future concepts and utilize the advanced technologies of an AAN force?

The Army might have to undergo a cultural shift from a more hierarchical organization to a flatter organization. Shifting from hierarchical to flatter forms of organization would be challenging, because too much decentralization could jeopardize unity of effort. The Army would have to balance the need for autonomous and even independent action with the need for central control.

Possible resolutions: Soldiers assigned to Battle Forces might have to remain in their positions longer than is currently the norm in combat units in order to assure a continuously high level of proficiency. The normal three-year tour with frequent job changes might cause too much turbulence. The Army recently began implementation of Operational Personnel Management System (OPMS) XXI that may address some of the observed problems. OPMS XXI is expected to lengthen tours and create an operational career field.

To achieve a flatter organization, the Army would have to re-examine and modify leader development for commissioned and noncommissioned officers.

Technological Implications

Training simulators, especially those simulating the operation of complex equipment, might help to achieve and maintain basic skills. Near-real-time displays and decision aids might permit more decentralized decisionmaking without affecting the unity of effort. In addition, new equipment might be highly modular, reducing the requirement for soldiers to develop complex technical skills.

Operational Implications

Less frequent reassignment of soldiers and a specialized career path comparable to a combat arm might be required to achieve and maintain proficiency. Very likely, Battle Force soldiers would be highly experienced soldiers, not soldiers on their first enlistment. Maintaining personnel of this quality would entail high additional costs. It is unclear to what extent soldiers in the Reserve Components could maintain skills at the levels required by a Battle Force. It seems unlikely that Battle Force units in the reserves could conduct high-intensity combat without postmobilization training, but the resulting delay would greatly reduce the utility of Battle Force units.

WHAT ARE APPROPRIATE ROLES FOR ARMY RESERVE AND NATIONAL GUARD FORCES?[14]

Game Play

During game play, National Guard heavy forces mobilized quickly and deployed without refresher training. Some game players questioned whether this standing start was realistic for Army XXI units in the Reserve Components.

Red directed attacks at infrastructure across the United States in the hope that state governors would insist on retaining National Guard units under their own command for home defense, making the units unavailable for deployment. But Blue was able to mobilize and deploy the limited number of National Guard divisions required to backfill in Korea and conduct protracted land operations in the Gulf region. The Blue President federalized many of the remaining National Guard units to conduct homeland defense. State governors (not played) presumably did not object to federalization because they anticipated that most federalized units would defend their home states and because they recognized that successful defense required an effort coordinated at the national level.

In the Red team, there was much discussion about Blue mobilization and deployment of units from its reserve component. Red players doubted that the Blue President would have decided to call up 200,000 reservists before Red began an overt invasion of Saudi Arabia. Moreover, Red players thought that rapid deployment of large Blue reserve and National Guard units without postmobilization training was unrealistic.

---

[14]Research Question 17, Reserve Component (RC) Combat Specialties: Should RC forces be trained for specialized missions such as urban conflict or peace-keeping? How might the RC develop a suite of AAN-era forces for stability operations as well as future conflict?

Possible resolutions: Units in the active component will probably have to "buy time" for National Guard combat forces to achieve full readiness.

Technological Implications

Advanced simulation might allow soldiers in the Reserve Components to achieve and maintain a higher level of skill than is currently possible.

Operational Implications

Homeland defense tends to blur the distinction between law enforcement and military operations. Military forces would undertake missions scarcely distinguishable from large-scale law enforcement and be constantly available to support law enforcement agencies in sudden emergencies that required the application of force. National Guard forces have a comparable mission to assure public order today, but arrangements vary from one state to another.

If the United States were under heavy attack by enemy agents and special operations forces, an administration might find it necessary to employ national collection assets within the continental United States. To assure its legal position, the administration would want enabling legislation that gave the President discretionary power during a national emergency. Even so, such a move might have serious political repercussions.

Chapter Five

OTHER ISSUES

The following issues might not directly affect decisions on the organization, equipment, and training of AAN forces, but they are of general interest to Army planners. We relate each issue to the research questions set for the 1998 SWG, explain how each issue emerged from game play, briefly explore possible resolutions, and suggest technological and operational implications.

WHAT AUTHORITY TO EMPLOY SPACE-BASED WEAPONS SHOULD NCA PREDELEGATE TO CINCSPACE?[1]

Game Play

Commander-in-Chief, Space Command (CINCSPACE) emphasized that Blue was dependent upon its space assets, was highly vulnerable to attack, and had little capability to reconstitute its space assets. Moreover, events could occur very quickly in space, leaving CINCSPACE little time for consultation. Therefore, players thought that the Blue President should take the prudent step of predelegating authority to CINCSPACE to respond when:

- Blue national security space assets were attacked from space.

- Blue satellites were threatened by a direct ascent missile.

[1]Research Question 7, Space Capabilities: How will space-based capabilities enable the conduct of operations in 2021? What space capabilities were used in the conflict? What actions did Red/Orange take to exploit these vulnerabilities?

- Blue homeland was attacked by submarine-launched missiles.

During these preliminary discussions, a difference in perspective became apparent. CINCSPACE was preoccupied with the military defense of Blue space assets. The Blue President understood the military dimension, but felt that CINCSPACE was not sufficiently sensitive to the political implications. The Blue National Security Advisor feared that Russia and China would respond to Blue actions, possibly causing an escalatory cycle.

When CINCSPACE presented his requests in writing, the Blue President made several predelegations. He authorized CINCSPACE to destroy any object in space that attacked Blue national security space assets, but not the entire constellation of related objects. Before attacking the entire constellation, CINCSPACE was to request permission from the Blue national command authority (NCA). He authorized CINCSPACE to destroy any direct ascent missile on the presumption that no country would fire such a missile unless it had hostile intent. He authorized CINCSPACE to destroy submarine-launched missiles that would impact on the Blue homeland on the presumption that such a launch would indicate either hostile intent or a dangerous accident. In all these cases, there might not be enough time for CINCSPACE to request and receive authority from the NCA before Blue suffered damage.

Possible resolutions: The NCA may have to predelegate authority to assure timely response in space. However, this authority should be carefully devised and periodically reviewed to minimize the risk of inadvertent escalation.

Technological Implications

To protect its national space assets, the United States would require a sensor suite for warning and space-based weapons capable of near-instantaneous response.

Operational Implications

Failure to respond quickly to attacks on U.S. space assets could lead to degradation of capabilities that are vital to AAN operations.

HOW COULD THE NCA PREVENT THIRD COUNTRIES FROM USING NUCLEAR WEAPONS AGAINST EACH OTHER?[2]

Game Play

India and Pakistan were engaged in a conflict over Kashmir and both countries were armed with nuclear weapons. The Blue President wanted to prevent the use of nuclear weapons for two basic reasons: First, any nuclear use would cross a threshold established in the international community since 1945 and possibly encourage further use. He described this phenomenon as "letting the genie out of the bottle." Secondly, an exchange between India and Pakistan might cause widespread damage that would have economic repercussions throughout the region and compel Blue to offer extensive humanitarian aid.

Blue decisionmakers recognized that the conflict was asymmetrical. India did not have to employ nuclear weapons because it enjoyed overwhelming superiority in conventional forces. In contrast, Pakistan relied on nuclear weapons as an ultimate guarantee of national survival.

The Blue President directed a diplomatic and military effort to deter and, if necessary, prevent use of nuclear weapons by India and Pakistan. He directed the Blue Secretary of State to advise both countries that Blue would intervene to prevent an exchange. He directed CINCSPACE to allocate a number of kinetic kill vehicles to an operation directed against missiles fired from Indian and Pakistani territory. (It is not clear whether the Blue NCA had considered that CINCSPACE would be unable to distinguish nuclear from conventional missiles.) He directed CINCEAST to employ airborne lasers for the same purpose and to conduct information operations to bring international pressure on India and Pakistan, detect the locations of their mobile launchers, and disrupt command and control associated with nuclear weapons. Blue military commanders estimated

---

[2]Research Question 7, Space Capabilities: How will space-based capabilities enable the conduct of operations in 2021? What space capabilities were used in the conflict? How did these assets enable or enhance Blue's ability to be decisive?

that they would be able to intercept and destroy about half of the missiles fired from Indian and Pakistan territory.

CINCEAST intercepted conventional ballistic missiles fired by both sides during offensive counterair operations. He intercepted many missiles successfully, but many also impacted. The net result was to put Pakistan, the weaker side, at a greater disadvantage. The unintended effect was to impel Pakistan toward an earlier use of nuclear weapons than might otherwise have been the case. In this sense, Blue's interception of ballistic missiles was counterproductive.

When Indian land forces penetrated deeply into the Punjab, Pakistan attacked the lead element with a small nuclear weapon delivered by aircraft. Since this use occurred on its own territory, Pakistan might also have used a land vehicle to deliver the warhead. Pakistan intended this action as a warning that it would use nuclear weapons as necessary to prevent further Indian advance.

Possible resolutions: It is questionable whether the United States could prevent other countries from using nuclear weapons if they had multiple delivery means. The United States probably could not physically interdict nuclear use, unless the belligerents were severely limited in available delivery means.

Instead of trying to interdict delivery, the United States might put its own weight into the balance by offering to side with the country whose national survival was at stake. A credible assurance that its opponent would cease military operations might obviate the motive to use nuclear weapons. However, this strategy might require greater involvement in the conflict than the American people would be willing to accept.

Technological Implications

The United States might require a flexible ballistic missile defense with potentially global reach. To attain global reach, this defense might have to be mounted in space. In addition, the United States might need readily deployable theater-level assets capable of dealing with atmospheric delivery means.

Operational Implications

The United States would have to establish national policy in advance of a potential nuclear exchange. This policy would probably have to include the level of effort the United States was willing to sustain and the desired end state, analogous to a conventional theater campaign. But U.S. national leadership might have difficulty justifying the risk inherent in such a policy to Congress and the American public.

HOW COULD THE NCA DISCOURAGE USE OF COMMERCIAL SPACE ASSETS TO AN ENEMY WHILE INCREASING ITS OWN CAPABILITY?[3]

Game Play

Although no adversary country had its own space assets, all were receiving space-derived information through contracts with space-capable nations, especially Russia. As Russia was not a party to the conflict, there were limited means to apply leverage to get it to stop providing information, and there was no basis for attacking its space-based systems. The satellites in question were not dedicated to Red but served multiple users. Blue wanted to reduce or eliminate the information that Red was receiving.

Possible resolutions: Some information operations personnel thought that it might be possible to prevent the transmission of one channel of information while leaving the rest of the satellite completely functional. This would allow the denial of the Red channel without affecting other users. After discussion, it was unclear whether this was possible and, if so, if it could be done in a deniable way.

---

[3]Research Question 7, Space Capabilities: How will space-based capabilities enable the conduct of operations in 2021? What space capabilities were used in the conflict? What was the impact of commercial space assets on the conduct of operations?

Technological Implications

Commercial space services are proliferating, and it is extremely likely that in a future conflict even a relatively unsophisticated opponent will receive some coverage through commercial space assets. If it is possible to deny part of the information from a satellite without turning it off completely, the United States should develop that capability. It will be especially useful if that capability can be made deniable, but that seems unlikely.

Operational Implications

Future opponents may be able to receive satellite data through commercial contracts and therefore have more intelligence on U.S. forces than the relative technological capability of the two countries would suggest. The United States may have difficulty denying use of commercial satellites. It may have difficulty discerning when data is being passed from commercial satellites, and targeting them might outrage owners and users.

UNDER WHAT CIRCUMSTANCES SHOULD THE NCA AUTHORIZE FIRST USE OF SPACE-BASED WEAPONS AGAINST TERRESTRIAL TARGETS?[4]

Game Play

During the course of the game, Blue attempted to reduce Red's capacity for command and control and to eliminate Red's weapons of mass destruction. One weapon available to attack especially hard targets was the hyper velocity rod fired from a satellite. The Blue NCA was reluctant to authorize weapons use from space but was finally convinced that some of the command and control facilities were too hardened to be effectively attacked by other means. The Blue team was convinced that such use did not violate any treaties and that the rods would not be considered weapons of mass de-

---

[4]Research Question 7, Space Capabilities: How will space-based capabilities enable the conduct of operations in 2021? What space capabilities were used in the conflict? How did these assets enable or enhance Blue's ability to be decisive?

struction. The NCA finally authorized the use, and a number of facilities were attacked with the rods. Other player teams were of the opinion that the Blue use did violate treaties, and some were of the opinion that the rods were weapons of mass destruction. The game ended without resolution of the issue.

Possible resolutions: The issue was more one of perception than of definition. It might be useful to be very specific about such weapons in international agreements, but there is also the argument that ambiguity can be useful in such cases.

Technological Implications

Deployment of kinetic-energy weapons in space appears to be technically feasible in the near future. The decision to develop such capability, however, is less technological than political. There is no point in such a deployment if it is not clear that these weapons could be used.

Operational Implications

If space-based weapons are deployed, operational commanders must be careful not to rely too much on their capability. The authorization to use space-based weapons may be fraught with as much hesitation as was seen in the game, and release may never come.

HOW SHOULD CIVILIAN AND MILITARY ORGANIZATIONS BE ORGANIZED AND CONTROLLED TO CONDUCT EFFECTIVE DEFENSE OF THE HOMELAND?[5]

Game Play

The Blue President responded to a Red campaign of sabotage and raids in the Blue homeland by organizing a Task Force led by the

---

[5]Research Question 16, Terrorism: How do we defend against foreign and domestic terrorism? What instances of terrorism occurred? What capabilities were employed or suggested for counterterrorism, including the use of RC units? What are the appropriate roles and missions for the RC and AC under the heading of homeland defense?

Deputy Attorney General. This Task Force was built around representatives of the Department of Justice and the Department of Defense with support from the national intelligence agencies. The Operations Support Team organized Joint Task Force (JTF) of the Americas to control military forces allocated to homeland defense. The Deputy Attorney General regularly reported during Blue National Security Council meetings concerning activities of the Task Force.

Blue decisionmakers debated several issues concerning homeland defense. As the Red campaign continued, the Deputy Attorney General requested authority to employ national collection assets within CONUS. It was debated whether the NCA should grant such authority on the basis of a finding or request enabling legislation from Congress. The second alternative was preferable in view of the ramifications for civil liberties. Another issue was federalization of National Guard units engaged in homeland defense. The Blue President and his National Security Advisor anticipated that state governors might object to federalization, preferring to retain control over their forces and assure defense of their own states. Finally, the Blue NCA was concerned that National Guard forces, with the exceptions of certain specialized units, might not have the training and equipment required to be effective.

Possible resolutions: In case of a concerted threat to the United States, the NCA might designate a lead agency or authorize an interagency working group to coordinate homeland defense. To achieve greater effectiveness, the NCA might authorize creation of a new entity that combined the efforts of civilian and military agencies.

Technological Implications

A new generation of wide-area sensors might be used to reduce the manpower required to guard key installations, such as power stations, seaports, and airports. Improved database technology might help to link federal, state, and local agencies, improving the ability to share information rapidly. Sensors able to detect nuclear, biological, and chemical agents might help to detect introduction of such weapons. The United States also would require redundant, secure communication links that are not normally used in peacetime, for example between the Federal Bureau of Investigation and military units, active and reserve. The United States would have to protect these links against cyber attacks and physical sabotage.

Operational Implications

Close cooperation would be required between civilian law enforcement and military forces. Indeed, the customary distinction between law enforcement and military operations might become blurred. To attain such cooperation, relationships between civilian and military agencies should be delineated and exercised in advance of crisis. Interplay of federal, state, and local authorities should also be understood in advance.

The United States would probably also want to establish close cooperation with authorities in third countries that might be used as bases or staging areas for attacks in CONUS.

Special operations forces would play an important role in homeland defense. To play this role, they might disperse to several locations, and the number of such forces might be expanded.

Chapter Six

RECOMMENDATIONS

DEVELOP A SPECTRUM OF CONCEPTS FOR THE NEW COMPONENT OF AAN

The Army should develop a spectrum of concepts for the new component of the Army After Next. Previous wargames tended to demonstrate advantages of the current air-mech concept, while the Spring Wargame tended to demonstrate limitations.

Advantages of the Current Air-Mech Concept

The current air-mech concept has these advantages:

Global self-deployment. In the current concept, air-mech forces deploy with organic tilt-rotor aircraft from their home bases into a theater of operations using combinations of intermediate staging bases and aerial refueling. These same tilt-rotor aircraft also provide operational and tactical mobility. Thus air-mech forces not only self-deploy at strategic distances, but also enter combat immediately without any requirement to disembark from air- or sealift and assemble. As a result, air-mech forces offer an unprecedented ability to introduce land forces anywhere in the world within days without dependence on sister services, other than Air Force tankers. This degree of strategic mobility approximates the global reach today associated only with air forces.

Vertical maneuver. Once in theater, air-mech forces use their organic tilt-rotor aircraft for operational and tactical mobility. Like today's airmobile forces, they can maneuver deep into an enemy's rear area, strike quickly, and recover before he can respond effectively. Rapid vertical maneuver thus affords air-mech forces a high degree of protection against slower-responding enemy forces. In contrast to today's airmobile forces, air-mech forces bring their own light (15-ton) armored vehicles into the fight, giving them far greater mobility on land and much greater firepower.

Precision fire. Air-mech forces not only have highly effective direct-fire weapons, but also advanced indirect-fire weapons that allow precise engagement at great depths. They combine mobility and firepower to spring "precision ambushes"[1] that disorient enemy forces, destroy their most important assets, and break their cohesion. Air-mech forces engage with devastating firepower at ranges that exceed an enemy's ability to respond effectively.

Limitations of the Current Air-Mech Concept

The current air-mech concept has these limitations:

Inability to fight in urban terrain. In the Spring Wargame, Red's use of urban terrain largely negated the effectiveness of air-mech Battle Forces. They could not attack into urban terrain to dislodge Red forces because the 15-ton combat vehicles were not sufficiently protected to risk close engagement. Nor could Blue air forces alone dislodge Red from cities. This mission fell to land forces that were heavier than Battle Forces and had greater dismounted strength, operating in partnership with tactical aviation. Such forces included Army XXI units together with Air Force elements, Marines supported by land- and carrier-based aviation, and allied contingents. This limitation of air-mech Battle Forces will become increasingly debilitating as more and more of the world's population concentrates in urban areas. Indeed, large portions of the earth's surface, including much key terrain, are already covered by urban sprawl. It is imperative that Army forces, including the early-arriving forces, be able to fight successfully in urban terrain.

---

[1] BG (ret.) H. Wass de Czege, "Future (2025) Joint Operations and Land Power Tactics," briefing dated March 1998.

Inability to hold ground. Air-mech Battle Forces are designed to conduct strike missions, then quickly relocate. They are not designed to seize and hold parts of the earth's surface against opposing forces designed for traditional land warfare. During the Spring Wargame, inability to hold terrain against Red's advancing forces was a limitation that contributed to Red's operational success. As an example, the Red force advancing toward Riyadh suffered severe air attacks in open terrain for two days and sustained heavy casualties, but it still reached and occupied the Saudi capital because no land forces blocked its way. During the first week of the campaign, Blue committed an air-mech Battle Force on just one occasion; a Battle Force attacked a 2020-pattern Red division that was advancing along the Gulf littoral toward Abu Dhabi. This Battle Force inflicted severe losses on the Red division, which nonetheless reached and occupied Abu Dhabi, where it linked up with Red forces that air assaulted across the Straits of Hormuz. After completing its strike, the Battle Force withdrew for its own safety rather than attempting to block the Red advance. In the absence of the Battle Force, Red's badly depleted division and a follow-on division continued to advance against Omani forces that were too weak to stop them. According to *Army Vision 2010:* "The power to deny or destroy is possessed by each of the military Services. The contribution of land forces to the joint warfight is the power to exert direct, continuing, and comprehensive control over land, its resources, and its people."[2] Forces designed according to an air-mech concept did not make this primary contribution of land forces in the Spring Wargame.

Vulnerability to air defense. The air-mech Battle Force is intended to strike at opposing heavy forces. The Spring Wargame suggested that such opportunities may be limited, in part due to opposing air defense. For example, Blue planners considered attacking Tehran early in the campaign but rejected this option. It was questionable whether Blue could have conducted such an attack successfully, because Red defended Tehran and other major cities in its homeland with well-protected land forces and very formidable air defenses. Even on the march, Red land forces enjoyed highly effective air defense. Due in part to the vulnerability of tilt-rotor aircraft, air-mech Battle Forces had limited options early in the campaign. Indeed,

---

[2]Department of the Army, *Army Vision 2010,* p. 2.

their only significant operation during the first week was a tactical strike against Red forces (as previously mentioned) that failed to achieve operational success. This game play suggested that air-mech Battle Forces might be ineffective unless air defenses were largely suppressed. Moreover, air defense suppression could be extremely difficult, especially as concerns low-altitude nonemitting systems, including guns and shoulder-fired missiles. During Desert Storm, in 1991, for example, the United States usually evaded low-altitude air defenses by flying outside their range, but Battle Forces might not have this option.

Alternative Concepts

Considering these limitations to the air-mech concept, the Army needs to develop and examine other concepts for its future forces. Like the air-mech concept, these concepts should be designed to win campaigns swiftly and decisively with minimal collateral damage. In the end, the Army might decide that the air-mech concept is most promising, but it cannot make an informed decision without examining alternatives.

Among the concepts that might be selected for more detailed study are:

Air/sea-lifted light armor force. Combat vehicles weighing 20–30 tons might have enough protection to accept close engagement in constrictive terrain. Vehicles in this weight class could be airlifted in sufficient numbers to operate successfully during the first days of a campaign.   Alternatively, this force might arrive by ultrafast (approximately 70 knots) sealift. Once in theater, it would operate on land at high speeds (approximately 80 mph) using wheeled propulsion.

Sea-lifted medium armor force. Combat vehicles weighing 25–40 tons (roughly half the current weight)[3] might have enough protection

---

[3]Dr. A. Fenner Milton, quoting Army Research Laboratory technical constraints, states that only vehicles exceeding 25 tons can survive rapid-fire, medium-caliber cannon and man-portable anti-armor weapons. See "Army After Next Proposal for Ground Combat Vehicles," briefing by Dr. A. Fenner Milton, Deputy Assistant Secretary for Research and Technology OASA (RDA), July 1998.

to assure successful engagement in constricted terrain and also dismount significantly greater numbers of infantry. Such forces would be too heavy for airlift unless much larger and more capable airlifters were developed. However, they could be sealifted, prepositioned, and forward deployed. At this weight, vehicles normally require tracks to achieve acceptable ground pressures and therefore would be appreciably slower.

STUDY DEPLOYMENT AND LOGISTICS SUPPORT

During the Spring Wargame, deployment and logistics received more attention than in previous wargames, but much work remains to be done. The Army needs to study these issues for the current air-mech concept and for other concepts as well. There may be little point in examining the operational utility of forces that could not deploy strategically or be sustained in theater as assumed.

Requirements for deployment of early-arriving forces need more scrutiny. For example, the air-mech concept may be limited by maximum-on-ground (MOG) restrictions at staging airfields and by the very large quantities of fuel required for a fleet of tilt-rotor aircraft. Willingness of allied and friendly nations to support deployment by granting bases and overflight permission might be critical. Finally, the availability of aerial refueling should be assessed, especially during the early phase of a campaign when air-mech forces might compete directly with air forces, both operational and strategic, for tanker assets.

Availability of fuel in theater could also be an issue, even on the Arabian peninsula. During the Spring Wargame, both Army and Air Force platforms would have required large amounts of fuel, presumably prepositioned. But these stocks and associated Saudi facilities were heavily damaged during Red's initial air operations.

Use of a Mobile Offshore Base (MOB) needs further examination.[4] During the Spring Wargame, a MOB was used for several different purposes by joint forces. The ability of a MOB to support several users simultaneously is not well understood. In fact, it is question-

---

[4]The MOB is described on p. 25, footnote 12.

able whether an entire air-mech Battle Force could base on a MOB even if it were entirely devoted to this single use.

EXPLORE WAYS TO COOPERATE WITH ALLIES

It is self-evident that the United States will not fight alone. In the past it did not fight alone, and it is even less likely to do so in the future. According to *Army Vision 2010:* "Land component operations in 2010 will be fully integrated with those of joint, multinational, and nongovernmental partners. Recent experience reminds us that Army operations have never been and never will be independent."[5]

During the Spring Wargame, allied contributions were critical, including those of regional allies and NATO partners. Without allied contributions, the Gulf States would have been overwhelmed before Blue could even halt Red forces, much less strike a decisive blow. Therefore it is important to understand how Army forces, especially conceptual forces developed in Army After Next, would operate in conjunction with allied forces despite dissimilarities in weapons and doctrine. There may also be circumstances in which an opponent would fight in coalition.

Army After Next wargames have tended to separate future Army forces from allied forces, leaving combined operations to Army XXI forces or sister services. But this separation may not make the best use of Army forces, especially during the first phase of a campaign when Red's chances of success are greatest. Instead, the Army needs to explore ways to enhance alliances by combining its forces with allies, including forces designed under futuristic concepts. Interoperability will be infeasible in many respects, but collaboration and even cooperation might well be possible and mutually beneficial.

In addition, future wargames might well include play of Red coalitions. During the Cold War, the Soviet Union was critically dependent upon its Warsaw Pact allies that were indifferent, disaffected, and sometimes openly rebellious.

---

[5]Department of the Army, *Army Vision 2010,* p. 10.

TRADOC RESEARCH QUESTIONS

1. Overseas/CONUS Balance. What are the considerations for balancing overseas presence and power projection to properly posture AAN forces for global maneuver?

- What Flexible Deterrent Options (FDO) did the Blue NCA consider and/or use?

- What types of forces demonstrated or suggested flexibility?

- What bases were denied to Blue by uncooperative allies?

- What negotiations took place to establish or reestablish basing rights?

- What conditions prevented the deployment of potentially useful forces from the continental United States (CONUS) or from a forward base? Example: Were units unable to leave Korea because China seemed threatening?

- What were the considerations for mobilizing/deploying Reserve Component forces?

- What were the assumptions about deployment times?

- How were deployment times impacted by decisionmaking?

- When did forces actually arrive?

2. Stability Operations. How do/what end state conditions affect the commitment of residual forces to maintain regional stability?

- What was the actual end state of the conflict versus the end state desired by the United States?

- What was the composition and mission of residual forces?

- What considerations drove this composition?

- What alternatives to residual forces were considered to maintain regional stability?

- What was the final disposition of military forces?

- What was the political, economic, and social disposition of the major contenders?

- What is the enemy capability to resume hostilities?

- What was the regional balance of power after the conflict?

3. Information Operations. How do we integrate the range of information operations into the campaign?

- In the context of this strategic setting, how did each operational CINC define information dominance?

- To what extent did Blue achieve information dominance at any point in any conflict, throughout the world or in localized areas?

- How long did it last? What stopped it?

- What elements of information operations were used during the campaign?

- How were these operations coordinated into the campaign?

- What was their impact?

- How was IO Bomb Damage Assessment (BDA) determined?

- How did IO affect the enemy's political will?

4. Relevant Ground Forces. In the context of joint and combined operations, how do we integrate and balance critical capabilities to create strategically and operationally relevant ground forces in 2021?

- What joint and/or combined operations occurred?

- What forces deployed and how quickly?

- What precluded successful, timely deployment?
- What capabilities of the ground forces were considered critical to the success or failure of the operation?
- To what extent were early-entry forces protected, sustained, and able to conduct decisive operations?
- What shortfalls or redundancies in capabilities were apparent in the conduct of simultaneous operations?

5. Interoperability. What essential characteristics and capabilities must AAN forces possess to ensure interoperability with joint, combined, or allied forces in 2021?

- What interaction did AAN forces have with joint, allied, or coalition forces?
- When and where did interoperability become critical?
- What interoperability problems occurred or were raised?
- What are the military (and potentially, political) effects of concept or capability mismatch between combined or coalition forces?
- How does this affect the CINC's organization for combat?
- What solutions were found to interoperability problems?

6. Pace. Given greater emphasis upon speed, mobility, and information, what is the impact of the pace of warfare on decision making in 2021?

- How did the strategic deployment capabilities of AAN forces affect the NCA decision to deploy forces?
- In what situations was en route planning critical to meet changing conditions?
- At conflict termination, what was the extent of post-conflict planning?
- To what extent did Red/Orange plan for operations beyond Blue's horizon?

- What actions did Red/Orange use to influence Blue's pace?

7. Space Capabilities. How will space-based capabilities enable the conduct of operations in 2021?

- What space capabilities were used in the conflict?
- How did these assets enable or enhance Blue's ability to be decisive?
- What is the origin of these capabilities, i.e., are they new or have they largely migrated to space from other domains?
- To what degree should AAN-era forces rely upon space-based and unmanned airborne vehicle (UAV) based assets at the expense of other systems investments?
- What critical vulnerabilities will AAN forces possess by a reliance on space-based capabilities?
- What actions did Red/Orange take to exploit these vulnerabilities?
- How did other countries support Blue's opponents with space capabilities?
- What was the impact of commercial space assets on the conduct of operations?
- Under what conditions did the loss of space or UAV assets or capability cause a mission failure?
- What other resources were available that might have prevented such a failure?
- Conversely, how did UAVs or space assets cover for the loss of other assets?

8. Urban Operations. What operational concepts should be used during the employment of AAN-era battle forces in large urban areas?

- How are the superior speed, mobility, and information capabilities of AAN-era forces affected by complex terrain consisting of large urban areas?

- What are the critical limitations and vulnerabilities associated with the employment of AAN-era battle forces in large urban areas?

- How did Red/Orange try to exploit complex terrain characteristics?

- What doctrinal, organizational, and technological enhancements are necessary to offset these limitations?

- How can the capabilities of AAN-era forces be used to reduce the requirement for soldier-intensive close combat tactical operations on urban terrain?

- What technologies and combat multipliers were useful in urban warfare?

- Which nonlethal or unmanned systems were useful?

- What character did Information Operations assume in an urban environment?

- What roles did coalition forces or civil authorities play?

9. Maneuver from Strategic Distances. Conceptually, what are the implications of conducting operational maneuver from strategic distances?

- What is the operational reach of AAN forces in this strategic setting?

- What were the problems encountered in protecting the force during the maneuver?

- How do you escort and protect high-speed transport ships?

- What were the apparent risks to decisive operations in dedicating scarce assets to force protection?

- What are the Command Control and Communications (C3), Deployability, Sustainability and Logistics (DSL) implications of operational maneuver from strategic distances?

- What were the shortfalls in force deployment and sustainment?

- What level of host nation support was available?

- What were the throughput capabilities of staging areas and intermediate staging areas?

10. AAN Concepts. What operational concepts and inherent capabilities prove most useful in combating major competitors in 2021?

- What capabilities are necessary to ensure land forces can execute missions across the full spectrum of conflict in 2021?

- What operational concepts were discussed or used against major competitors?

- How effective were these concepts and capabilities perceived to be?

- With respect to the full spectrum what kinds of conflict occurred?

- What concepts and capabilities were perceived as critical for success?

11. AAN Flaws. What are the conceptual flaws to AAN forces that can be exploited?

- What types of capabilities were not available to AAN forces that would have permitted more effective employment?

- What investments appear to have less utility than expected?

- Which missions did AAN forces have difficulty accomplishing?

- What additional capabilities were needed?

- How did competitors exploit operational approaches of AAN forces?

12. Scarcities. What critical capabilities become scarce during employment against multiple contingencies?

- Under what conditions were resources unavailable due to commitment in other theaters or operations?

- What were the effects of any shortfalls in satellite coverage, air and missile defense coverage, airlift and sealift?

- Under what conditions were communications capabilities inadequate?

13. Emerging Threats. What capabilities and characteristics might emerge during the next twenty-five years that a competitor could craft into a significant operational concept within his own strategic context that would pose a challenge to AAN forces?

- What technologies emerged that threatened AAN forces?

- What operational concepts could counter AAN capabilities?

- What innovative organizational characteristics pose a threat?

14. Asymmetries. What are the potential vulnerabilities of AAN forces to asymmetric counters?

- Which asymmetric counters might future adversaries pursue, as demonstrated in this conflict?

- What capabilities are required to counter or protect against asymmetric actions?

15. Fog and Friction. To what extent will information technologies affect "fog" and "friction"?

- What shortfalls in situational awareness were experienced, especially due to widespread contingencies?

- To what extent was the fog of war dispelled for AAN forces?

- How effective were any attempts to increase the enemy's "fog"?

16. Terrorism. How do we defend against foreign and domestic terrorism?

- What instances of terrorism occurred?

- What are the impacts of foreign and domestic terrorism on our ability to defend the homeland?

- What capabilities were employed or suggested for counterterrorism, including the use of RC units?

- What are the appropriate roles and missions for the Reserve Component and the Active Component under the heading of homeland defense?

- What are the impacts of terrorism on AC/RC integration?

- How effective were attempts at counterterrorism?

- How effective was international cooperation?

17. Reserve Component Combat Specialties. Should RC forces be trained for specialized missions such as urban conflict or peace-keeping/making?

- How might the RC develop a suite of AAN-era forces for stability operations as well as future conflict?

- How extensive is the variety of operations in which the RC can be expected to maintain proficiency?

- Which missions involving long-term RC deployment would be acceptable to the American public?

- In what special missions did AAN forces participate?

- Are any of these missions appropriate for RC level of training?

18. Reserve Component at Echelons Above Battle Force. What is the appropriate "enabling" role for RC units within Echelon Above Battle Force organizations?

- What roles did Reserve Component units play?

- What roles were perceived as critical?

- What roles did they *not* play, due to mobilization time lines?

- In what roles (unplayed) could they have been effectively used?

- What are potential roles for individual Reserve Component personnel (as opposed to Reserve Component units)?

- What role does the deployment of reserve forces play in gaining national support?

19. Emerging Issues. Analysts are likely to identify emerging issues that do not fall in the scope of the issues identified by DCSDOC and listed above. Analysts should document these issues, citing the nature of the issue and the conditions under which the issue surfaced. All emerging issues will be reviewed by the analysis integration team to determine common themes.

REFERENCES

1. M. D. Millot, W. Perry, and B. Pirnie, *The Army After Next: Strategic Objectives and Issues for High Level War Games,* Santa Monica, CA: RAND, PM-582-A, September 1996.

2. *Army After Next Spring Wargame, State of the World 1998–2021,* TRADOC, 19–30 April 1998.

3. A*rmy After Next 1998 Spring Wargame, Game Book,* TRADOC, 19–30 April 1998.

4. W. L. Perry and M. D. Millot, *Issues from the 1997 Army After Next Winter Wargame,* Santa Monica, CA: RAND, MR-988-A, April 1998.

5. *Analysis Plan for the Army After Next Spring Wargame 1998,* TRADOC Analysis Center, 8 April 1998.

6. W. Perry and B. Pirnie, *The Army After Next Spring Wargame: Initial Impressions,* Santa Monica, CA: RAND, PM-809-A, April 1998.

7. *Army Vision 2010,* Department of the Army (undated).

8. *Emerging Impressions from the AAN Spring Wargame 1998,* TRAC, May 1998.

9. *Integrated Analysis Report, AAN Winter Wargame 1997,* TRAC, May 1997.

10. *Army After Next 1998 Spring Wargame Political-Military Workshop Game Book,* TRADOC, March 1998.

11. BG (ret.) H. Wass de Czege, "Future (2025) Joint Operations and Land Power Tactics," briefing dated March 1998.

12. *AAN 1998 Spring Wargame Political Military Workshop: Workshop Guide,* TRADOC, 22–24 March 1998.

13. "Army After Next Proposal for Ground Combat Vehicles," briefing by Dr. A. Fenner Milton, Deputy Assistant Secretary for Research and Technology OASA (RDA), July 1998.